Praise for

HALFWAY HOME

"Halfway Home is wonderful! A fascinating mixture of travelogue, family and self-discovery done in a unique and entertaining way."
—Jeff Smith, author of the *Bone* series

"Christine's Japan travelogue reaches back to your own young travels and transports you alongside her to the wonderful bliss of that era of discovery and adventure. Full of good food and hilarious observations, Christine tells her story with the wit and pen of someone well beyond her years, while still capturing what it is to be sixteen and checking out cute boys on the subway."
—Lucy Knisley, author of *French Milk*

"In this beautifully illustrated memoir, Christine Inzer takes us to Japan for an unforgettable summer vacation. Along the way, she gets attacked by hungry deer, eats very un-French crepes, and finds salvation ... in the form of a vending machine. Like Japan itself, *Halfway Home* is mouth-watering, funny, and moving."
—Matthew Amster-Burton,
author of *Pretty Good Number One: An American Family Eats Tokyo*

"I laughed out loud! The art is great, and the observations very smart. This is the perfect book for anyone visiting Japan for the first time."
—Hiroko Yoda,
co-author of *Ninja Attack! True Tales of Assassins, Samurai, and Outlaws*

"A charming and impressive debut. Christine Inzer is one to watch."
—Hope Larson, author of *Mercury*

HALFWAY HOME

HALFWAY HOME

DRAWING MY WAY THROUGH JAPAN

Written and Drawn by
Christine Mari Inzer

Published by Naruhodo Press

NARUHODO PRESS
www.naruhodopress.com

Copyright © 2014 by Christine Mari Inzer

Library of Congress Control Number: 2014916150

ISBN   978-0-9907014-0-8

Each day is a journey, and the journey itself home.

— Matsuo Bashō,
The Narrow Road to the Deep North

CONTENTS

INTRODUCTION

DURING THE SUMMER OF 2013, JUST BEFORE I TURNED 16, I SPENT EIGHT WEEKS IN JAPAN VISITING MY GRANDPARENTS AND GETTING REACQUAINTED WITH MY BIRTHPLACE.

WHILE IN JAPAN, I VISITED MY FAVORITE SPOTS IN TOKYO THAT I HADN'T SEEN IN YEARS, AND I ALSO TRAVELED TO THE CITY OF KYOTO FOR THE FIRST TIME.

THIS BOOK IS A COMPILATION OF DRAWINGS, SKETCHES, AND COMICS I MADE WHILE IN JAPAN.

THE TITLE REFERS TO MY SOMEWHAT FEELING HALF AT HOME IN BOTH JAPAN AND AMERICA, BEING BORN TO PARENTS OF BOTH COUNTRIES.

MY SUMMER IN JAPAN WAS AN INCREDIBLE EXPERIENCE, AND I HOPE TO SHARE SOME OF THAT WITH YOU.

ABOUT ME

MY MOTHER IS FROM JAPAN

MY DAD IS FROM AMERICA

AND THIS IS ME

BORN IN JAPAN BUT RAISED IN AMERICA

I IDENTIFY MYSELF AS AN ASIAN-AMERICAN, BUT I ALWAYS TAKE CARE TO NOTE THAT I HAVE ONLY ONE ASIAN PARENT. SO I AM LITERALLY ASIAN AND AMERICAN, EVEN THOUGH MOST ASIAN-AMERICANS ARE FULLY ASIAN BUT LIVE IN AMERICA... AS UH... AMERICANS.

THIS IS IT.

I'M AT THE AIRPORT. I'VE
CHECKED MY BAG AND I'M
GETTING READY TO SAY
GOODBYE TO MY FAMILY.

DARK

(DYED)
BROWN
HAIR

LIGHT

SOME
ARTSY
FARTSY
SHIRT

BRAND
NEW
BACKPACK!

↑
SWATCH

SHAPELY
YOGA
PANTS

NEW CONVERSE!

I MADE IT!
I'm at the GATE

FIRST I SAID MY FAREWELLS TO MY FAMILY.

ADIEU

MY SISTER CRIED & MADE ME SAD. I ALMOST CRIED WHEN I HUGGED MY DAD.

THEN I WENT TO SECURITY AND GOOFED UP A COUPLE TIMES.

THE LAPTOP HAS TO BE BY ITSELF IN A BIN.

OH SHOOT

LAPTOP   JACKET

AND I FORGOT TO TAKE OFF MY SHOES.

SWEETIE YOU NEED TO TAKE YOUR SHOES OFF.

WHY AM I FORGETTING EVERYTHING?

BUT I GOT THROUGH AND I'M OK.

UP IN the air

I HAD A TRANSCENDENTAL MOMENT ON THE PLANE, EATING MY HÄAGEN-DAZS ICE CREAM AND LISTENING TO CAMILLE SAINT-SAENS' DANSE MACABRE.

The ice cream was very hard

OH, BY THE WAY, I'M ON THE PLANE RIGHT NOW.
IT'S REALLY HARD TO TELL WHAT TIME OF DAY IT IS, AND I CAN'T SLEEP.

IT'S STILL 7 HOURS TILL THE PLANE ARRIVES, BUT I'M ALREADY WONDERING WHAT I'M SUPPOSED TO DO WHEN I GET OFF THE PLANE (MY DAD TRIED TO WALK ME THROUGH IT, BUT I FORGOT WHICH ORDER IT'S SUPPOSED TO GO IN).

IF I SPOKE JAPANESE BETTER, I WOULD NOT BE AS ANXIOUS (ALTHOUGH I GET ANXIOUS EASILY).

EARLIER I WAS WORRIED ABOUT THE PLANE TOILETS
(see illust. for further explanation)

The toilet is so small

Me in toilet

PRESSURE

THIS IS TAKING SO LONG

I'M JEALOUS B/C MY SEAT NEIGHBOR LOOKS SO PEACEFULLY ASLEEP

The Traveler

I DID NOT SLEEP ON THE PLANE... I ONLY HAD ONE HOUR OF SLEEP BEFORE BEING AWAKENED BY PASSENGERS OPENING WINDOW SHADES AND LETTING LIGHT FLOOD THE PLANE. I AM TIRED, SWEATY, AND FIGHTING TO HOLD BACK MY FEAR. BUT GETTING OUT TURNS OUT TO BE REALLY EASY... THE CUSTOMS OFFICIAL BARELY GLANCES AT MY PASSPORT BEFORE HE WELCOMES ME TO JAPAN.

OVERALL, I HAD BEEN HOPING FOR A MORE GLAMOROUS ENTRANCE, BUT I COULDN'T EVEN ROLL MY SUITCASE PROPERLY. THIS IS WHAT I WANTED

WEHH

Weary Traveler

MAKE WAY FOR THAT GIRL WHO LOOKS LIKE SHE KNOWS WHAT SHE'S DOING!

I KNOW WHAT I'M DOING

SHE KNOWS WHAT SHE'S DOING

Ideal Traveler

THE ARRIVAL GATE AT NARITA

STARTING IN...

KASHIWA

柏

KASHIWA IS WHERE MY GRANDPARENTS
LIVE. IT'S A SMALL CITY JUST
OUTSIDE OF TOKYO.

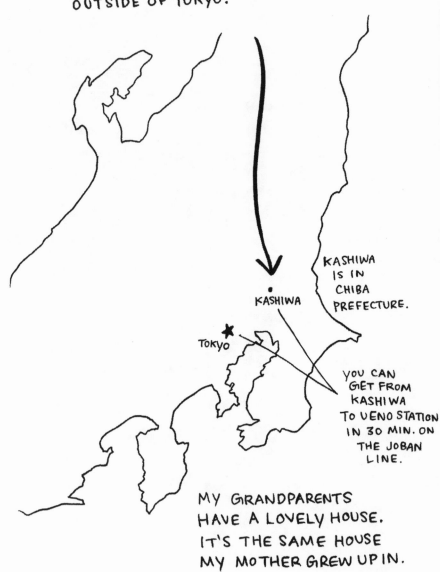

KASHIWA
IS IN
CHIBA
PREFECTURE.

• KASHIWA

★ TOKYO

YOU CAN
GET FROM
KASHIWA
TO UENO STATION
IN 30 MIN. ON
THE JOBAN
LINE.

MY GRANDPARENTS
HAVE A LOVELY HOUSE.
IT'S THE SAME HOUSE
MY MOTHER GREW UP IN.

This is
BABA
MY GRANDMA.

AND THIS IS
JI JI

WHILE I WAS IN
JAPAN, I STAYED
WITH MY GRAND-
PARENTS. BABA
AND I, AS YOU'LL
SEE IN THIS BOOK,
DID ALMOST EVERY-
THING TOGETHER.

MY GRANDPA. EVERY
SUMMER HE GOES OFF
INTO THE YAMAGATA
MOUNTAINS FOR A FEW WEEKS
TO COOL OFF AND GO FISHING.

IT'S MY THIRD DAY

MY AUNT AND COUSINS ARE HERE. THEIR NAMES ARE MEGU, TAIGA
& KAREN. THEY'RE LIVING IN INDIA RIGHT NOW AND ARE VISITING TOO.
I'M TOLD I'M A LOT LIKE MY AUNT MEGU. WE'RE BOTH VERY
DIFFERENT FROM MY MOTHER (AKA MEGU'S OLDER SISTER, AYUMI)
AND I THINK THAT MAKES US SIMILAR TOO. MY MOTHER IS LESS...
CONVENTIONAL.

- FAIRER
- TALLER
- SLENDER
- LIVES IN INDIA
- TAKES AFTER
  MOTHER
- THE GOOD CHILD

- TANNER
- SHORTER
- ATHLETIC
- LIVES IN USA
- TAKES AFTER
  FATHER
- TROUBLEMAKER

YOU REALLY WOULDN'T THINK THEY WERE PRODUCED
BY THE SAME TWO PEOPLE,
BUT I LIKE IT THIS WAY.
IT MAKES LIFE MORE INTERESTING.

14

TRENDY TEENAGERS

I WENT TO THE KASHIWA STATION MALL WITH BABA TODAY.
IT HAS ONE BUILDING WITH A LOT OF STORES FOR YOUNG, HIP
PEOPLE, AND I REALLY LIKE IT. IT'S CHEAP TOO.
IT WAS VERY INTIMIDATING THOUGH TO
STAND AROUND THE GIRLS WORKING THERE.

THIS HAT STYLE IS POPULAR

DUMBAS

AND OF COURSE THEY HAVE PERFECTLY DYED, SHINY HAIR AND LOADS OF EYE MAKE-UP

VIVID GRAPHIC TEES

I BOUGHT a bag that says California despite having no connection to the state whatsoever. I'd be flattered if someone thinks I'm a
❀ Cali gurl ❀

SAW A GIRL WEARING THIS FOR REAL

THIS IS THE BEST OUTFIT I BROUGHT.

FLOWER JEANS ARE EVERY-WHERE

OF COURSE THEY WEAR HEELS!
THEY TOWERED OVER ME... UGH!

Yum Yum Yum

BESIDES MY GRANDPARENTS, THE SECOND GREATEST REUNION I HAD IN JAPAN WAS WITH A CERTAIN FAST FOOD CHAIN YOU CAN'T FIND IN AMERICA...

MOS BURGER

THE LOVE OF MY LIFE. I'LL SHOW YOU WHAT A MOS BURGER IS:

GIANT SLICE OF TOMATO

SPECIAL RELISH SAUCE

DICED ONIONS

BEEF PATTY

IT'S SERVED IN THIS WRAPPER AND YOU MUST EAT IT WITH THE WRAPPER BECAUSE NO ONE TAKES IT OUT OF THE WRAPPER. THAT WOULD BE WEIRD AND MESSY.

BATHTIME

AKA THE ONE ELEMENT OF JAPANESE CULTURE I COULDN'T HANDLE

LOOK, HERE'S THE THING. IN JAPAN, YOU DON'T EVER TAKE BATHS **LIKE THIS:**

THERE ISN'T ANY SOAP IN THE TUB. YOU DO NOT WASH YOURSELF IN. THE. TUB.

INSTEAD, YOU WASH YOURSELF OUTSIDE THE TUB. **LIKE THIS:**

① RINSE SELF BY POURING A BUCKET OF WATER ON SELF

② LATHER SOAP ON SELF LIKE A SUPERSTAR

③ RINSE AGAIN— DUMP THAT WATER BUCKET OVER SELF

YOU DO ALL OF THIS BEFORE YOU GET INTO THE TUB.

I TRIED TO DO IT.

DRENCHED IN WATER

BUT HERE'S WHAT THEY DON'T TELL YOU...

IT'S SO COLD

LUCKY FOR ME, MY GRANDPARENTS ALSO HAD A SHOWER.

HYSTERICAL
IN
HARAJUKU

I WANTED

TO GO INTO THE CITY –
BY MYSELF.
AT FIRST, MY GRANDMA
SAID **NO**
BUT
I SAID
YES!
I'M **BIG** ENOUGH!

I'VE SEEN
8-YEAR-OLDS
BOARD THE
TRAIN...
I CAN DO
IT, FOR SURE.
AFTER SOME
COAXING BY MY
MOM, MY GRANDMA
SAID **OK**
EVEN THOUGH I
KNOW SHE THOUGHT
I WOULD GET LOST,
GET KIDNAPPED,
GET HURT, GET
MURDERED!??!!
BRING IT.
BUT WHERE DO I GO...?

WE DECIDED ON HARAJUKU, BECAUSE IT WAS EASY TO GET TO AND DIDN'T HAVE MANY "CREEPY" PEOPLE, WHICH WAS MY GRANDMOTHER'S MAIN CONCERN...

THE PLAN WAS (PRETTY) SIMPLE.

AND THEN I WAS ON THE TRAIN, REALIZING THERE WAS NO TURNING BACK -!

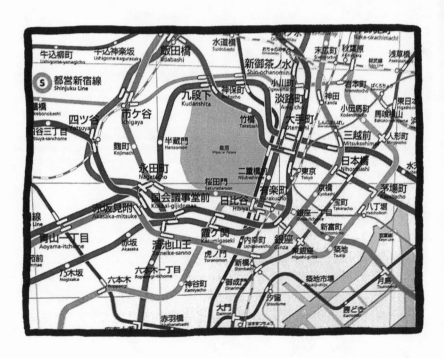

NOW STOPPING

WHEN I GOT OFF THE TRAIN AT HARAJUKU STATION,
I NEEDED TO USE THE BATHROOM. I STUMBLED INTO
THE FIRST STALL AND ...

SECOND STALL...

THIRD STALL (there's only 4)

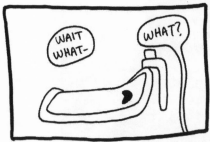

25

THEN AND NOW

TOKYO CREPES

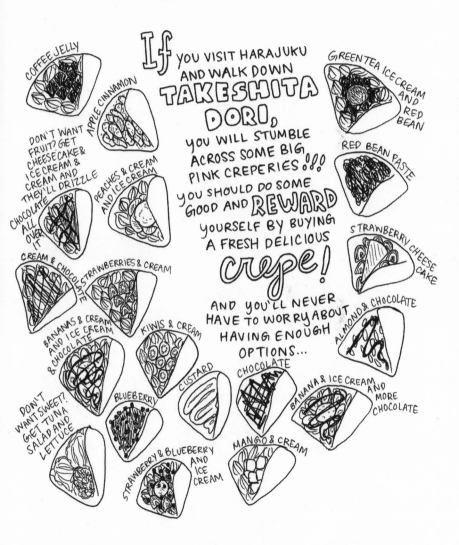

If you visit Harajuku and walk down **TAKESHITA DORI**, you will stumble across some big pink creperies!!! You should do some good and **REWARD** yourself by buying a fresh delicious *crepe!* And you'll never have to worry about having enough options...

COFFEE JELLY

APPLE CINNAMON

DON'T WANT FRUIT? GET CHEESECAKE & ICE CREAM & CREAM AND CHOCOLATE ALL OVER IT

PEACHES & CREAM AND ICE CREAM

GREEN TEA ICE CREAM AND RED BEAN

RED BEAN PASTE

STRAWBERRY CHEESECAKE

CREAM & CHOCOLATE

STRAWBERRIES & CREAM

BANANAS & CREAM AND ICE CREAM & CHOCOLATE

KIWIS & CREAM

CUSTARD

CHOCOLATE

ALMOND & CHOCOLATE

BANANA & ICE CREAM AND MORE CHOCOLATE

DON'T WANT SWEET? GET TUNA SALAD AND LETTUCE

BLUEBERRY

STRAWBERRY & BLUEBERRY AND ICE CREAM

MANGO & CREAM

MODEL SCOUT OR PERVERT?

31

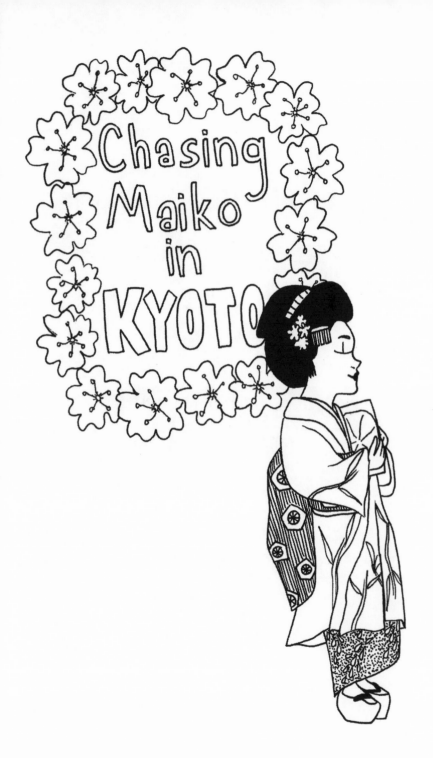

Chasing
Maiko
in
KYOTO

A RIDE ON THE shinkansen
新幹線

ALSO KNOWN AS THE BULLET TRAIN! MY GRANDMOTHER AND I RODE IT TO GET TO KYOTO, AND IT ONLY TOOK THREE HOURS. IF WE USED A NORMAL TRAIN, IT WOULD HAVE TAKEN MUCH LONGER. THE INTERIOR IS ALSO OBVIOUSLY A LOT NICER.

I LIKED THE VIEW. MAINLY JUST ROOFTOPS OF SMALL HOUSES AND STRETCHES OF GREEN FARMLAND AND MOUNTAINS. BUT WE DIDN'T GET TO SEE MT. FUJI BECAUSE IT WAS TOO CLOUDY!

THERE WAS A BUSINESS MAN ACROSS THE AISLE WHO LOOKED VERY TIRED AND UPSET ☹

WHAT I ATE TODAY

AFTER WE ARRIVED IN KYOTO, BABA AND I CHECKED INTO OUR HOTEL AND FOUND A NICE TONKATSU PLACE NEARBY. TONKATSU IS A POPULAR DISH IN JAPAN, CONSISTING OF BREADED PORK SERVED WITH CABBAGE AND A SPECIAL SAUCE.

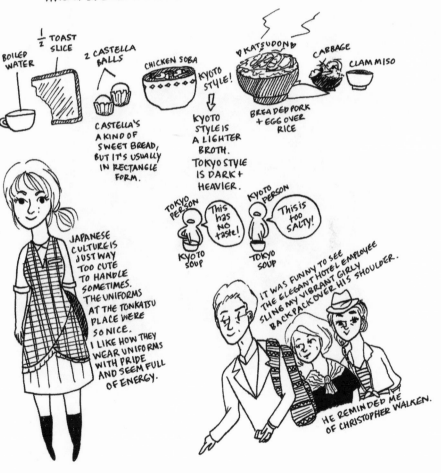

BOILED WATER

½ TOAST SLICE

2 CASTELLA BALLS

CASTELLA'S A KIND OF SWEET BREAD, BUT IT'S USUALLY IN RECTANGLE FORM.

CHICKEN SOBA

KYOTO STYLE!

KYOTO STYLE IS A LIGHTER BROTH. TOKYO STYLE IS DARK + HEAVIER.

♡ KATSUDON ♡

BREADED PORK + EGG OVER RICE

CABBAGE

CLAM MISO

TOKYO PERSON — This has NO taste!

KYOTO SOUP

KYOTO PERSON — This is too SALTY!

TOKYO SOUP

JAPANESE CULTURE IS JUST WAY TOO CUTE TO HANDLE SOMETIMES. THE UNIFORMS AT THE TONKATSU PLACE WERE SO NICE. I LIKE HOW THEY WEAR UNIFORMS WITH PRIDE AND SEEM FULL OF ENERGY.

IT WAS FUNNY TO SEE THE ELEGANT HOTEL EMPLOYEE SLING MY VIBRANT GIRLY BACKPACK OVER HIS SHOULDER.

HE REMINDED ME OF CHRISTOPHER WALKEN.

ON OUR FIRST FULL DAY IN KYOTO,
MY GRANDMOTHER AND I
WENT TO

KINKAKU-JI

ALSO KNOWN AS THE
"TEMPLE OF THE GOLDEN PAVILION".
IT IS A ZEN BUDDHIST TEMPLE,
FAMOUS FOR ITS SHINING GOLDEN
EXTERIOR AND ITS GARDEN LAYOUT.

THIS THING
AT THE TOP
IS A GOLDEN
PHOENIX.

ON THIS
LEVEL
YOU CAN
SEE
THE INTERIOR.

THIS IS A CLOSE-UP OF THE GOLDEN PHOENIX ON TOP OF KINKAKU-JI :

KIND OF CREEPY LOOKING, NO...?

WHEN I REMARKED ON HOW NEW KINKAKU-JI LOOKED, I LEARNED THE KINKAKU-JI I WAS LOOKING AT WAS A **RECONSTRUCTION.** THE ORIGINAL WAS **BURNT DOWN** BY A CRAZY BUDDHIST MONK.

DRAWN AT THE KINKAKUJI
TEMPLE

IT WAS *REALLY* CROWDED.
THERE WERE LOTS OF SCHOOL
GROUPS VISITING.

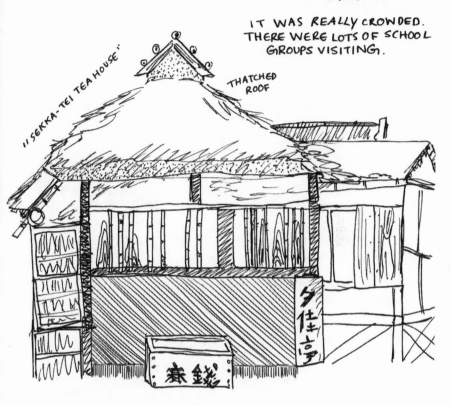

"SEKKA-TEI TEA HOUSE"

THATCHED
ROOF

I'M PRETTY SURE I COMMITTED A BUDDHIST
CRIME TODAY THOUGH WHILE TRYING TO
DRAW THIS:

AN ANT CRAWLED
ONTO MY LEG AND
I FREAKED OUT
AND KILLED IT.

GOMEN.

NEXT: **RYOANJI**

outline of some of the rocks

I THINK I SHOULD TRY AND DO SOME TRANSCENDENTAL THINKING/WRITING, BEING IN ONE OF JAPAN'S MOST FAMOUS HISTORICAL SIGHTS, BUT THE CAMERA CLICKS AND TOURISTS (I KNOW, I KNOW, I'M ONE MYSELF) MAKE IT KIND OF HARD TO BE ENLIGHTENED.

I'M NOT GOING TO TRY AND DRAW THE ROCK GARDEN. IT'S SOMETHING YOU HAVE TO SEE FOR YOURSELF. THERE ARE 15 ROCKS. FROM WHERE I SIT I CAN COUNT 13.

NOW SOMEONE JUST SAID THERE ARE 14. NOPE, THERE ARE 15.

I'M SUPPOSED TO FEEL GOD OR BUDDHA'S SPIRIT. WHAT DO I SEE?

- I SEE THE PROFILE OF A MAN'S FACE
- I CAN DEFINITELY SEE THE ROCKS AND MOSS AS ISLANDS IN A GRAVEL OCEAN
- A FOOT?
- I'M NOT VERY GOOD AT THIS
- APPARENTLY YOU'RE SUPPOSED TO BE IN A ZEN STATE TO VIEW THE ROCK GARDEN CORRECTLY SO WOOPS

Lotus & lilypads from the landscape garden

PEOPLE I'VE SEEN REPEATEDLY TODAY

YOUNG JAPANESE COUPLE ON THE BUS

SCHOOLGIRL I THINK I SCARED AND I FEEL BAD

PERSON I CAN ONLY RECOGNIZE BY HER CLOTHES

RED SKIRT & CROCS

FABULOUS KOREAN BOYS — I SAW ONLY THE BACK OF THEIR HEADS

THIS GUY'S COLLAR WAS POPPED UP

THE ROCKS OF RYOANJI

I FOUND THE GEISHA!

THE GION DISTRICT IN KYOTO IS ONE OF THE FEW PLACES IN JAPAN WHERE YOU CAN SEE A GEISHA. IN THE EARLY EVENING, IF YOU'RE IN THE RIGHT PLACE, YOU CAN SPOT THEM WALKING TO THE OCHAYA (TEAHOUSES) WHERE THEY ENTERTAIN.

MY DAD TOLD ME IT WAS ESSENTIAL TO SEE A GEISHA WHEN IN KYOTO. HE SEARCHED ONLINE AND TOLD ME I MIGHT HAVE LUCK NEAR THE TATSUMI-BASHI BRIDGE. SO IN THE EARLY EVENING, BABA AND I WAITED THERE, CAMERAS IN HAND.

HAVING NO LUCK AT THE BRIDGE, WE WALKED TO HANAMIKOJI STREET, AND VOILA, THE GEISHA APPEARED. TO BE CORRECT, THEY WERE ACTUALLY MAIKO, OR APPRENTICE GEISHA.

I KNEW IN ADVANCE THAT THEY WERE GOING TO WALK QUICKLY, BUT NOW I REALIZE IT'S NOT TO GET TO THEIR APPOINTMENTS ON TIME, BUT TO NOT BE MOBBED BY TOURISTS LIKE ME WHO WANT THEIR PHOTO.

There is the maiko that will sort of acknowledge your presence and faintly smile and look super pumped.

There is also the sort of scary maiko that simply looks down and walks down the street and ignores everything.

MAIKO MAYHEM

A maiko is an apprentice geisha. They get invited to entertain at parties, primarily dancing.

Many young girls who wish to take the first step to geisha-dom audition for JNTM ↪ JAPAN'S NEXT **topmaiko**

I'M TYRA BANKS & THIS IS CYCLE 10 OF...

YOU MUST HOLD THIS SCALDING HOT TEA CUP FOR 30 MIN

WORK IT! C'MON! BE FIERCE!

Beat Takeshi also hosts the annual Geisha Games, where Maikos must out-beautify (or kill) each other. Winner becomes Japan's most respected geisha.

Everything in this comic is 100% true.

NARA

(1 HOUR FROM KYOTO)

IN NARA, MY GRANDMA AND I WENT TO SEE THE DAI BUTSU - AKA GIANT BUDDHA - AT TŌDAI-JI TEMPLE. IF YOU EVER VISIT NARA, YOU WILL EVENTUALLY COME HERE BECAUSE *EVERYBODY* DOES. IT IS PACKED. I'D DRAW THE BUDDHA, BUT THAT WASN'T THE MOST EXCITING EVENT OF THIS VISIT - IT WAS THIS PILLAR.

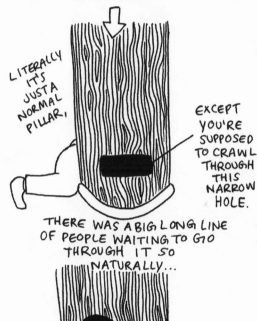

LITERALLY IT'S JUST A NORMAL PILLAR,

EXCEPT YOU'RE SUPPOSED TO CRAWL THROUGH THIS NARROW HOLE.

THERE WAS A BIG LONG LINE OF PEOPLE WAITING TO GO THROUGH IT SO NATURALLY...

CHEESE!

MY GRANDMA TOLD ME THAT CRAWLING THROUGH IT WAS GOOD LUCK, SO I DID IT BUT LATER WE FOUND A MONK AND QUESTIONED HIM ABOUT THE PILLAR'S SIGNIFICANCE...

BABA AND THE MONK

THE DEER IN NARA

My favorite tourists

(WHILE IN KYOTO)

① LOVELY AUSTRALIANS I TALKED TO IN A STARBUCKS!

THEY WERE JUST A BIT OLDER THAN ME, PROBABLY HIGH SCHOOL SENIORS OR COLLEGE FRESHMEN.

THEY ALL WERE FRIENDS JUST VISITING JAPAN! WHEN I'M OLDER, I PLAN TO DO THIS...

② ATTRACTIVE, ARTISTIC-LOOKING YOUNG FOREIGN (I say this b/c they were not conversing in English) COUPLE

Babe lets blow dis taco joint

Probably what they were saying

He had silvery hair!

THEY WERE NOT AFRAID OF DISPLAYING THEIR AFFECTION. I LIKED GLARING AT THEM.

③ THIS OLD LADY ON THE ESCALATOR. I ONLY EVER SAW THE BACK OF HER HEAD.

Blonde mohawk

Chain earring

"Unleash pain peaceful World"

UNLEASH PAIN PEACEFUL WORLD!

SHE WAS JAPANESE, AND HAD THE SWEETEST, PUREST VOICE. IT WAS A LITTLE WORN OUT FROM AGE.

④ TOTALLY RANDOM GROUP OF SMOKING HOT FRENCH GUYS ON THE BUS — THEY WOULDN'T SHUT UP EVER!

I'm going to stare at your butts the whole ride

Oui oui je suis beau croissant merde

Nous irons au «Kiyomizo?» Bla bla bla

AS A FRIEND ONCE PUT IT, MAYBE "I JUST HATE BEAUTIFUL YOUNG PEOPLE".

50

THE PROBLEM WITH JAPANESE BOYS

WHEN WE GOT BACK TO KASHIWA,
IT WAS TIME FOR MATSURI...

柏 まつり

KASHIWA   MA - TSU - RI !

MASKS

WATAME

To get one, you have to take a strip of paper tied to a fishhook and get the fish hook thru the yoyo's handle. If the paper gets wet the hook will fall.

THE KASHIWA MATSURI IS 2 DAYS LONG AND ATTRACTS AROUND 60 THOUSAND.

THESE ARE THE SORTS OF THINGS YOU'LL FIND AT EVERY MATSURI:

yoyo balloons THESE ARE MY FAVORITE THINGS. I ALWAYS MAKE SURE TO GET ONE.

Fish in bags
I HATE THIS GAME SO I DON'T PLAY IT. YOU HAVE TO PICK UP A FISH WITH THIS NET THAT'S MADE OF PAPER AND IT ALWAYS BREAKS.

GRUNTING GUYS CARRYING THIS DOWN THE STREET

I didn't get to see this up-close

YAKISOBA

OKONOMIYAKI

KAKIGORI

OK THE SHRINE IS TOO BIG BUT YOU GET THE PICTURE

YAKITORI   TAKO

IKA

SAKANA

THEY ALSO HAVE LITTLE LOTTERIES AND YOU PAY LIKE ¥500 AND PULL OUT A NUMBER THAT DETERMINES WHAT KIND OF PRIZE YOU WIN.

LITERALLY WINS THE BIGGEST PRIZE EVERY TIME

I SEE HOW IT IS ...

2 PACK OF MAGNETS

THE BEST AND WORST PART IN THE ART BALLET SEGMENT WAS THEM DANCING TO LADY GAGA'S "LOVEGAME" FOR THEIR FINALE.

SEXUAL INNUENDO

BUT MY FAVORITE PART OF MATSURI WAS THE **DANCERS!!!**

I GUESS I WAS THE ONLY ONE TO GET IT B/C NO ONE ELSE WAS LAUGHING.

WTF

"ART BALLET" DANCERS: THEY WEREN'T EVEN THAT GOOD AT DANCING BUT THEY HAD AWESOME COSTUMES. EVERYBODY WAS WONDERING WHAT ART BALLET MEANT. TURNED OUT TO BE BELLY DANCING WITH INDIAN MUSIC?

"YOSAKOI" DANCERS: MAINLY MIDDLE-AGED
よさこい LADIES DANCING TO UPBEAT MUSIC THAT MIXES NEW AND OLD JAPANESE MUSIC TOGETHER. IT LOOKS REALLY COOL WHEN IT'S CHOREOGRAPHED WELL. I WAS VERY IMPRESSED. IT LOOKS FUN.

MAKES CLACKING SOUND

I have a weak spot for cute boys and flags

57

THE FAMILY ARRIVES

MY FAMILY
They arrived yesterday

MY DAD
who is American

My MoM
who is Japanese

MY SISTER
who got really,
REALLY tan
and also
looks a
little older

MY BROTHER
Who grew
2 inches &
is starting to
eerily look like
a teenager...!!!
People say
we have very
similar faces.

HE ALSO REFUSED TO HUG ME

I DIDN'T REALLY MISS MY FAMILY UNTIL IT DAWNED ON ME THAT THEY WERE COMING, AND I'D GET TO SEE THEM. SOME THING THAT I HAVEN'T CONFESSED YET IS IT'S PRETTY LONELY HERE, AND I'M LOOKING FORWARD TO DOING THINGS IN JAPAN WITH THEM, AS A FAMILY.

ALSO, IT'S VERY EXCITING TO THINK I'LL BE STROLLING AROUND TOKYO WITH MY FAMILY, JUST LIKE WHEN I WAS LITTLE!

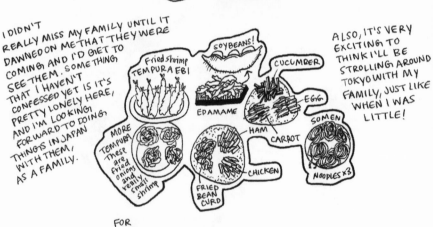

Fried shrimp
TEMPURA EBI

SOYBEANS!

EDAMAME

CUCUMBER

EGG

MORE TEMPURA These are fried onions and really small shrimp

HAM

CARROT

SOMEN

CHICKEN

FRIED BEAN CURD

NOODLES x3

FOR DINNER WE HAD **SOMEN**.
THIS IS HOW YOU EAT IT:

① HERE IS YOUR CUP W/SOMEN SOUP.

② PUT IN YOUR CHOICE OF MEAT/ VEGETABLES.

③

DUNK OR SOAK NOODLES AND THEN _ENJOY!_

IT'S TIME TO EXPLORE ...

(TOKYO)

Tsukiji

WAKE UP, WE'RE GOING TO つきじ!!

5 AM

つきじ - TSU-KI-JI IS THE WORLD'S BIGGEST FISH MARKET (ACCORDING TO MY DAD). EVERY MORNING STARTING AT 5 AM, THEY AUCTION OFF FRESH FISH TO SHOPS AND RESTAURANTS. THE PRICE OF FISH WORLD-WIDE IS BASICALLY DETERMINED HERE DAILY AT THE AUCTION. MY DAD WOKE UP THIS MORNING AND DECIDED ON THE SPOT HE WANTED TO GO AND SEE IT, LEADING TO MY UNPLEASANT AWAKENING.

IT WAS 5 AM, AND I WAS ALREADY SWEATING WHEN WE LEFT THE HOTEL. THE HEAT RIGHT NOW IS UNBEARABLE. I'M PRETTY SURE SOMEONE CAN DIE TODAY FROM THE HEAT. TODAY, THOUGH, I TRIED REALLY HARD TO NOT COMPLAIN, SO I TRIED THE "TAKE A DEEP BREATH AND CLOSE YOUR EYES" METHOD WHENEVER MY DAD TOOK PICTURES. I DO BELIEVE MY SANITY CRACKED THOUGH WHEN WE CAME TO THE MARKET AND HEARD THIS:

SORRY! RESERVATION WAS FULL AT 4:20.

COME MONDAY AT 4.

← HAPPY OLD MAN THAT WE COULDN'T GET MAD AT BECAUSE HE WAS SO NICE.

YOU WOKE ME UP AT 5 AM. 5. AM. FOR. NOTHING.

CHRISTINE STOP

NO

BEHAVE YOURSELF

VELOCIRAPTOR SCREECH

BUT THEN WE FOUND A 24 HR SUSHI PLACE NEARBY AND ATE FRESH SUSHI AT 6 AM.

WHAT I ATE:

CHU TORO
↳ MEDIUM FATTY TUNA

AKAMI
↳ REGULAR TUNA

SALMON

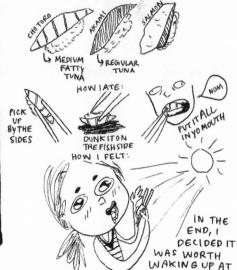

HOW I ATE:

PICK UP BY THE SIDES

DUNK IT ON THE FISH SIDE

PUT IT ALL IN YO MOUTH

NOM

HOW I FELT:

IN THE END, I DECIDED IT WAS WORTH WAKING UP AT 5 AM.

ASAKUSA

I WENT TO ASAKUSA AND KAMINARIMON TWICE: FIRST WITH JUST MY DAD,
THEN WITH MY ENTIRE FAMILY. KAMINARIMON IS A VERY FAMOUS GATE
LEADING TO A TEMPLE AND BASICALLY EVERYONE STANDS IN FRONT OF IT
AND TRIES TO TAKE A PICTURE. SINCE I JUST WENT TO KYOTO, I WAS
NOT THAT IMPRESSED BY IT, EXCEPT FOR ITS *HUGE* LANTERN.

KAMINARIMON MEANS "THUNDER GATE"

WE WALKED UP TO THE TEMPLE AND DID THE USUAL TOURIST-Y THINGS
(THERE WERE A LOT OF TOURISTS) AND THEN WE LEFT TO FIND FOOD.
ON OUR WAY TO THE RESTAURANT, WE RAN INTO THIS TOTALLY CRAZY LADY — SHE
WOULD STOP AND TALK TO ANYTHING MOVING ON THE STREET. SHE WAS REALLY
FRIENDLY, AND IT SEEMED LIKE SHE WAS JUST LOOKING OUT FOR EVERYONE.

SOBA

FOR LUNCH WE HAD ZARU SOBA AND TEMPURA

AND

WE SAT ON PILLOWS LIKE THIS

SOUP

TEMPURA

It was delicious

IMAGINE IT. A HOT SUMMER AFTERNOON. THE SUN BEATS DOWN RELENTLESSLY ON YOU. YOU'RE ON A BLAZING CITY SIDEWALK WITHOUT ANY SHADE. YOU'RE SWEATING EVERYWHERE AND IT'S GROSS. YOUR THROAT IS PARCHED. AND THEN YOU SPOT THIS IN THE DISTANCE:

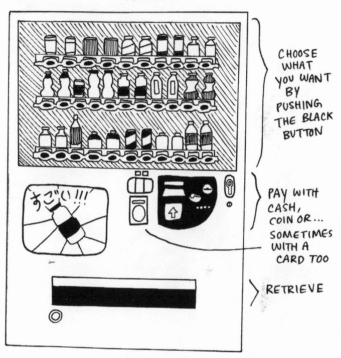

CHOOSE WHAT YOU WANT BY PUSHING THE BLACK BUTTON

PAY WITH CASH, COIN OR... SOMETIMES WITH A CARD TOO

RETRIEVE

ANGELS SING IN THE DISTANCE
IN JAPAN, YOU CAN ALWAYS COUNT ON FINDING A VENDING MACHINE SOMEWHERE - BECAUSE THEY'RE PRACTICALLY EVERYWHERE. I THINK PEOPLE EXPECT TO FIND MORE OF THE WEIRD* ONES THEY HEAR ABOUT, BUT MOST OF THEM JUST HAVE COLD DRINKS... TYPICALLY TEA, ICED COFFEE, JUICE, AND SPORTS DRINKS.

* I'VE HEARD ABOUT VENDING MACHINES THAT SELL UNDERWEAR

Maidtown

WENT TO AKIHABARA

WEIRDLY, THIS PLACE HAS THE MOST "POP CULTURE" STUFF, BUT IT WAS MY LEAST FAVORITE PLACE TO VISIT. I JUST... I WASN'T REALLY KEEN ON THE WHOLE SUBMISSIVE ANIME DREAM GIRL THING THEY HAD GOING ON. I DON'T HAVE ANYTHING AGAINST ANYONE WHO LIKES ANIME/MANGA! BUT UH... UH... I'M JUST NOT USED TO IT.

IT CERTAINLY WAS INTERESTING THOUGH. ONE THING I DID NOT SEE ANYWHERE ELSE WERE THE "MAIDS" ON THE SIDEWALKS PROMOTING THEIR MAID CAFÉS! THEY WERE FUN TO SEE, BUT I FELT SO BAD BECAUSE IT WAS SO HOT AND A LOT OF PEOPLE JUST WALKED PAST THEM (AS DO MOST PEOPLE WITH ANYONE HANDING OUT ANYTHING).

OK AS YOU CAN TELL I CAN'T DRAW ANIME/MANGA VERY WELL...

HM.

PLEASE JUST COME TO THE DAMN CAFÉ

HA HA HA

COME

HIIIII

HEE HEE

HIII

HI!

Levels (sic)

ON SUNDAYS AT YOYOGI PARK, YOU MIGHT HAPPEN TO STUMBLE UPON A GROUP OF SHIRTLESS MIDDLE-AGED MEN WITH MAGNIFICENT GREASED HAIR DANCING TO OLD-TIMEY ROCK AND ROLL. THESE ARE THE ROCKABILLIES, AND THEY'VE BEEN DANCING HERE AT YOYOGI SINCE MY FATHER FIRST CAME AS A STUDENT...

MY QUEEN

THE LEADER

HE DOESN'T REALLY DANCE, BUT HE HANDLES THE MUSIC.

AIR GUITAR

HE DIDN'T LOOK LIKE THE REST OF THEM, BUT HE WAS IN THEIR GROUP. THEIR WIVES AND KIDS CAME TO WATCH, AND HE AND ONE OF THEIR DAUGHTERS WENT TO THE VENDING MACHINE SO HE COULD BUY HER AN APPLE JUICE.

71

HACHIKO

(AKA GET READY TO CRY YOUR EYES OUT)

THIS IS **HACHIKO**. WELL, IT'S REALLY A STATUE OF HIM. ↳

YOU CAN FIND HIS STATUE AT SHIBUYA STATION. YOU MIGHT BE WONDERING WHY THERE EVEN IS A STATUE DEDICATED TO A DOG. THIS IS WHY:

THIS IS HACHIKO'S OWNER, HIDESABURO UENO, WHO COMMUTED TO WORK FROM SHIBUYA STATION.

EVERY DAY, HACHIKO WOULD WAIT IN FRONT OF SHIBUYA STATION FOR HIS OWNER TO RETURN FROM WORK. ONE DAY, UENO DID NOT RETURN. HE HAD SUFFERED A STROKE AND PASSED AWAY.

BUT HACHIKO CONTINUED TO COME TO THE STATION EACH AND EVERY DAY UNTIL HIS OWN DEATH 9 YEARS LATER. HE WON JAPAN'S HEART AND SO THEY MADE THIS STATUE IN HIS HONOR.

I CANNOT BELIEVE I HAVE NOT TALKED ABOUT RAMEN YET.

I'VE MENTIONED IT, PROBABLY, BUT HAVE I GIVEN IT ITS OWN PAGE YET?
BECAUSE IT NEEDS ONE.
I LOVE RAMEN. I EVEN LOVE TO DRAW IT.

NORI (SEAWEED)
BAMBOO
SOFT BOILED EGG
PORK
GREEN ONION

THIS IS WHAT A TYPICAL RAMEN HAS.

I THINK RAMEN IS BEAUTIFUL BECAUSE IT IS SO COMMON. YOU CAN FIND DECENT RAMEN ANYWHERE IN JAPAN. EVERYBODY EATS IT. I SEE CONSTRUCTION WORKERS EATING IT DURING THEIR LUNCH BREAK, THEN I SEE MOVIE STARS IN PHOTOS EATING—YOU GUESSED IT, RAMEN. IF THERE IS ANY RITE OF PASSAGE TO VISITING JAPAN, IT'S PROBABLY TO HAVE A BOWL OF RAMEN.

GOING HOME

THIS IS IT.

THE BRUTAL REALIZATION HIT ME
ONLY THE DAY BEFORE: I HAVE
TO GO HOME.

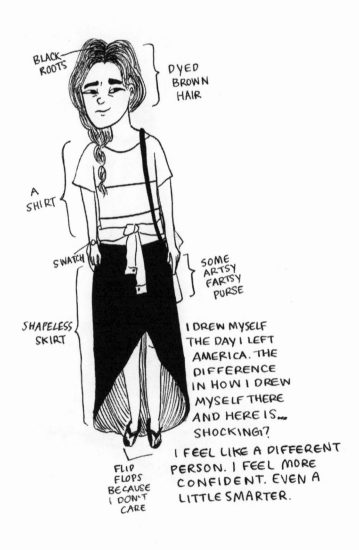

BLACK ROOTS

DYED BROWN HAIR

A SHIRT

SWATCH

SHAPELESS SKIRT

SOME ARTSY FARTSY PURSE

I DREW MYSELF THE DAY I LEFT AMERICA. THE DIFFERENCE IN HOW I DREW MYSELF THERE AND HERE IS... SHOCKING!?

I FEEL LIKE A DIFFERENT PERSON. I FEEL MORE CONFIDENT. EVEN A LITTLE SMARTER.

FLIP FLOPS BECAUSE I DON'T CARE

DID I **CRY?**

YES. AS USUAL. I'VE NEVER PUT MUCH THOUGHT INTO WHY THOUGH. JUST SAYING I'M SAD DOESN'T EXPLAIN IT.

I'M SAD, BUT NOT BECAUSE I DON'T WANT TO LEAVE. I WILL MISS IT, BUT I ALSO WANT TO GO HOME. WHAT WAS MOST PAINFUL WAS WHEN THE TRAIN DOORS CLOSED, AND BABA WAS STANDING OUTSIDE. AND ALSO, THE SCENERY OUTSIDE THE WINDOW, OLD HOUSE ROOFTOPS AND RICE FIELDS AND EVERYTHING SO VIVID WITH COLOR AND I WAS PASSING BY ALL OF IT FOR THE LAST TIME. I FELT THIS BIG LUMP IN MY THROAT AND A SWELL IN MY CHEST LIKE YOU GET WHEN SOME INDESCRIBABLE EMOTION GRABS A HOLD OF YOU. AND THOSE TWO THINGS, MY GRANDMA AND THE WINDOW, MADE ME CRY.

Be happy

AND DON'T FORGET THIS MOMENT EVER

♡ THINGS I LOVE ABOUT JAPAN ♡

Waiting for the light to turn green at Shibuya crossing in the early evening.

Ramen. Enough said.

People watching on the Yamanote line.

The Wind-Up Bird Chronicle by Haruki Murakami.

Street fashion on Takeshita-dori in Harajuku.

Mosburger.

Looking down at the maze of streets that is Tokyo from the top of Skytree.

Tower Records in Shibuya.

Stacking empty plates at kaiten-zushi.

The Japanese habit of apologizing for everything — something I recognize in myself.

Lunch at Homeworks in Hiroo, where we used to go when I was little.

Botchan by Natsume Soseki.

Mister Donut.

Totoro by Hayao Miyazaki.

Buying fresh sashimi in the late afternoon with Baba for dinner.

ACKNOWLEDGMENTS

I'd like to thank the following people who in one way or another helped me to write this book.

To my mother Ayumi, who always knew what to say to keep me focused on finishing this book.

To Baba and JiJi, my Japanese grandparents, who let me stay with them all summer and made my experience in Japan possible. I especially want to give my love to Baba, for showing me around Tokyo and Kyoto, for her delicious meals, and for keeping me company so I never felt alone.

To the Terajima family, aka my aunt Megu, uncle Ryota, and two precious cousins Taiga and Karen, who made my stay fun and helped me feel at home in Kashiwa.

To BlaBla and Pepaw, my American grandparents, for their unlimited love and support.

To my brother Stefan and sister Zoe, who drive me crazy most of the time, but whom I love nonetheless.

To all of my teachers. I'm quiet in class, but I hope my voice sings clear to you in this book.

To my friends and peers. Over the years you have been telling me to do something with my artistic passion... so here it is!

I sent an advance copy of the book to a number of authors and comic artists I respect and admire. I was overwhelmed by the response I received. Their feedback and suggestions were invaluable and helped me to make a better book. To them, arigato gozaimasu!

Finally, thanks to my publisher, who sat next to me one afternoon and convinced me to fly to Japan and write this book in the first place, who urged me to seek out exciting experiences during my trip, who offered suggestions and encouragement when I got stuck, who tirelessly corrected my grammar and edited each and every page, and who constantly assured me that I could finish this book when I felt like I couldn't. He also happens to be my father. Thanks dad.

ABOUT THE AUTHOR

Christine Mari Inzer was born in Tokyo in 1997 to an American father and a Japanese mother. She spent her first years in Japan until her family relocated to the US in 2003. She is now a high school senior in a small town in Connecticut.

Visit her website at www.christinemari.com